Dinosaur A-Z

Written by Simon Mugford
Designed by Jo Rigg

priddy books
big ideas for little people

A is for Allosaurus

meat-eater

friends.

huge,
sharp

eat

big

long

Say my name: al-oh-SAWR-us

B is for

crocodile-like jaws

Dinosaur height: 10 ft

My name is Baryonyx, which means 'heavy claw.' I like to eat smaller dinosaurs but my **favorite** food is fish. I catch them with my claws and then chew them up with my jagged teeth!

96 sharp, jagged teeth

strong claws useful for catching fish

Baryonyx

Say my name: BAH-ree-ON-iks

C is for coelophysis

jagged teeth

Dinosaur height: 7 ft

My name means 'hollow-boned,' and I am small and light. This means I can run very fast, which is useful for chasing things to eat and getting away from those who want to eat me.

long, thin neck

sharp claws

Say my name: SEE-low-FIE-sis

D is for Diplodocus

Dinosaur height: 26 ft

small head

28-foot long neck

45-foot long, whip-like tail

big, heavy feet

I am one of the longest dinosaurs that ever lived. I eat plants, but I can't chew very well, so I swallow huge stones that mash up the food in my enormous stomach.

Say my name: dih-PLOD-uh-kus

E is for Euoplocephalus

tail club to swing at attackers

bony horns around its head

armored back for protection

I don't eat other dinosaurs, but I can stop myself from being eaten! My back is covered with hard, bony plates and I have a big, heavy club at the end of my tail.

Say my name: YOU-oh-plo-SEF-ah-lus

Dinosaur height: 7 ft

F is for

thick, flexible neck

Dinosaur height: 2 ft

beak-like mouth

I am only about 3 feet long, but I have strong arms and hands that help me grab the leaves that I like to eat. I've got **strong legs,** and can run away from danger quickly.

long legs for running fast

sharp claws

Fabrosaurus

Say my name: FAB-roh-SAWR-us

G is for Gravitholus

bashing heads

long, stiff, heavy tail

Dinosaur height: 15 ft

We have very **thick** skulls, and that's why the other dinosaurs call us 'bone-heads.' We like to charge into each other headfirst, but sometimes it gives us a headache!

clawed feet

thick, rounded skull

Say my name: GRA-vith-OH-lus

H is for

duck-like beak

Dinosaur height: 20 ft

I'm often called 'duck bill' because my mouth looks like a beak. I have very small, flat teeth inside my cheeks, which I use to chew the plants that I like to eat.

flexible neck

Hadrosaurus

Say my name: HAD-roh-SAWR-us

I is for

sharp thumb spike

sharp, toothless beak

Wherever I go, I always meet other **Iguanodons** because there are lots of us around! I use the bony spike on my thumb to defend myself if someone starts a fight.

powerful legs

Iguanodon

Say my name: Ig-WAN-oh-DON

Dinosaur height: 18 ft

J is for Janenschia

I'm about **80 feet** long — pretty cool, right? With these bony plates on my back, I don't have to worry about **predators**. I eat a lot and I stand on my rear legs to reach the leaves in very high trees.

long neck for reaching food in trees

tough, bony plates across the back

very strong legs to support its weight

Dinosaur height: 56 ft

30-foot long tail

Say my name: yah-NEN-chee-ah

K is for Kentrosaurus

bony plates

sharp spikes

My name means 'prickly reptile.' I guess that's because of these spikes along my back and tail — they are there to protect me. I have a very small brain so I'm not the smartest dinosaur.

small head and brain

L is for

head crest

walks on four legs

My name means 'slender-horned face.' I'm about 6 feet long and I have this really cool-looking head crest and a little horned beak to bite my food.

beak

Dinosaur height: 2½ ft

Leptoceratops

Say my name: LEP-to-SEH-ruh-tops

M is for

powerful flippers for swimming fast

While those dinosaurs are walking around on land, eating boring old plants or even each other, we sea reptiles spend our time swimming and eating fish. I have these great flippers that help me swim fast.

Length: 15 ft

sharp, jagged teeth for catching fish

Macroplata

Say my name: mack-roh-PLAH-tah

N is for Nodosaurus

My **armor-plating** has given me my name — it means 'lumpy reptile.' Those knobbly plates on my back are really tough and it takes a lot to hurt me. I eat plants that are close to the ground.

fully-armored back and tail

small, narrow head and pointed snout

Dinosaur height: 10 ft

Say my name: NODE-oh-SAWR-us

O is for

long, spiny sail along its back

Dinosaur height: 15 ft

The 'sail' on my **back** is very helpful — I let the sun shine on it to warm me up. To cool down, I turn the sail into the wind and let it blow on my back.

four fingers and a spiked thumb

Ouranosaurus

three-toed feet

Say my name: oo-RAHN-oh-SAWR-us

P is for

long, hollow head crest

short, stiff tail

knobbly-textured skin

It may look **weird**, but that big tube on top of my head comes in useful. I can blow through it to make a really loud noise and warn my friends if I see anything dangerous.

Dinosaur height: 13 ft

Parasaurolophus

Say my name: PAR-ah-sawr-OL-oh-fus

Q is for Quetzalcoatlus

I am a **flying** reptile that lived at the same time as the dinosaurs. I am the **biggest** of my **kind** and the largest creature ever to fly. I like to eat fish, but sometimes I scavenge for scraps of meat.

18-foot long wings

three, sharp, claw-like fingers

7-foot long legs

long, thin toothless beak

Wing span: 36 ft

Say my name: KET-sal-koh-AT-lus

R is for Riojasaurus

small head with large eyes

long neck

I am one of the oldest of all the plant-eating dinosaurs and the first to have a long **neck**. I have big, heavy, strong legs and my bones are very solid and thick. I am about 36 feet long.

Dinosaur height: 17 ft

15-foot long tail

Say my name: ree-OH-ha-SAWR-us

S is for

very large eyes

Dinosaur height: 7 ft

I am a very smart dinosaur and I have very good eyesight, which helps me when I'm out hunting for food. People also call me 'Troodon,' but I prefer Stenonychosaurus.

sharp claws

bony spikes along its back

long, stiff tail

Stenonychosaurus

Say my name: ste-NON-ik-oh-SAWR-us

T is for

two long horns

one short horn

Dinosaur height: 13 ft

I live in a herd with other Triceratops. If any other dinosaurs try to hurt us, we bash into them as hard as we can, using the three sharp horns on our heads.

sharp beak for cutting up plants

bony neck plate

Triceratops

Say my name: tri-SEH-ruh-tops

U is for Ultrasaurus

Of all the long-necked, plant-eating dinosaurs, I am the biggest. I am about the height of a four-story building — whatever that is. I have an unusual crest on the top of my head and that's where my nostrils are.

30-foot long neck

bony head crest and nostrils

small mouth and teeth

Dinosaur height: 50 ft

18-foot long tail

V is for

sharp, curved teeth

tail that helps with balance

long, sharp claw

powerful jaws to tear through prey

Dinosaur height: 4 ft

I am one of the scariest dinosaurs around — my name means 'speedy predator.' We hunt in packs, using the sharp claws on our middle toes to catch our dinner!

Velociraptor

Say my name: va-LOSS-ah-RAP-tor

W is for

hard, flat skull

short arms

stiff tail and bulky body

I am a lot smaller than my crazy cousin Gravitholus, and my head isn't quite as thick, but I still like to use it to play head-banging games with my friends!

Wannanosaurus

Say my name: wah-NAN-oh-SAWR-us

X is for

knobbly back and neck

two horns above the eyes

long, stiff tail

strong legs

Dinosaur height: 22 ft

I am a big, meat-eating dinosaur. Those little horns above my eyes and the spikes on my back might seem a little strange, but I don't care — they make me look scary!

Xenotarsosaurus

Say my name: zeen-oh-TAR-soh-SAWR-us

Y is for

Dinosaur height: 18 ft

bony plates along back and tail

I use the plates on my back to warm myself by facing them toward the sun and cool down by turning away from it. I protect myself with these really sharp spikes on my tail.

small head

Yingshanosaurus

Say my name: YING-shan-oh-SAWR-us

Z is for Zephyrosaurus

Dinosaur height: 4 ft

strong jaws, with teeth in the cheeks

I am small, I eat plants and I can run pretty **fast.** My long tail helps me to keep my balance, and that makes running quickly a lot easier. I really like my name — it means 'west wind reptile.'

long tail

five-fingered hands

long rear legs

Say my name: ZEF-ih-roh-SAWR-us

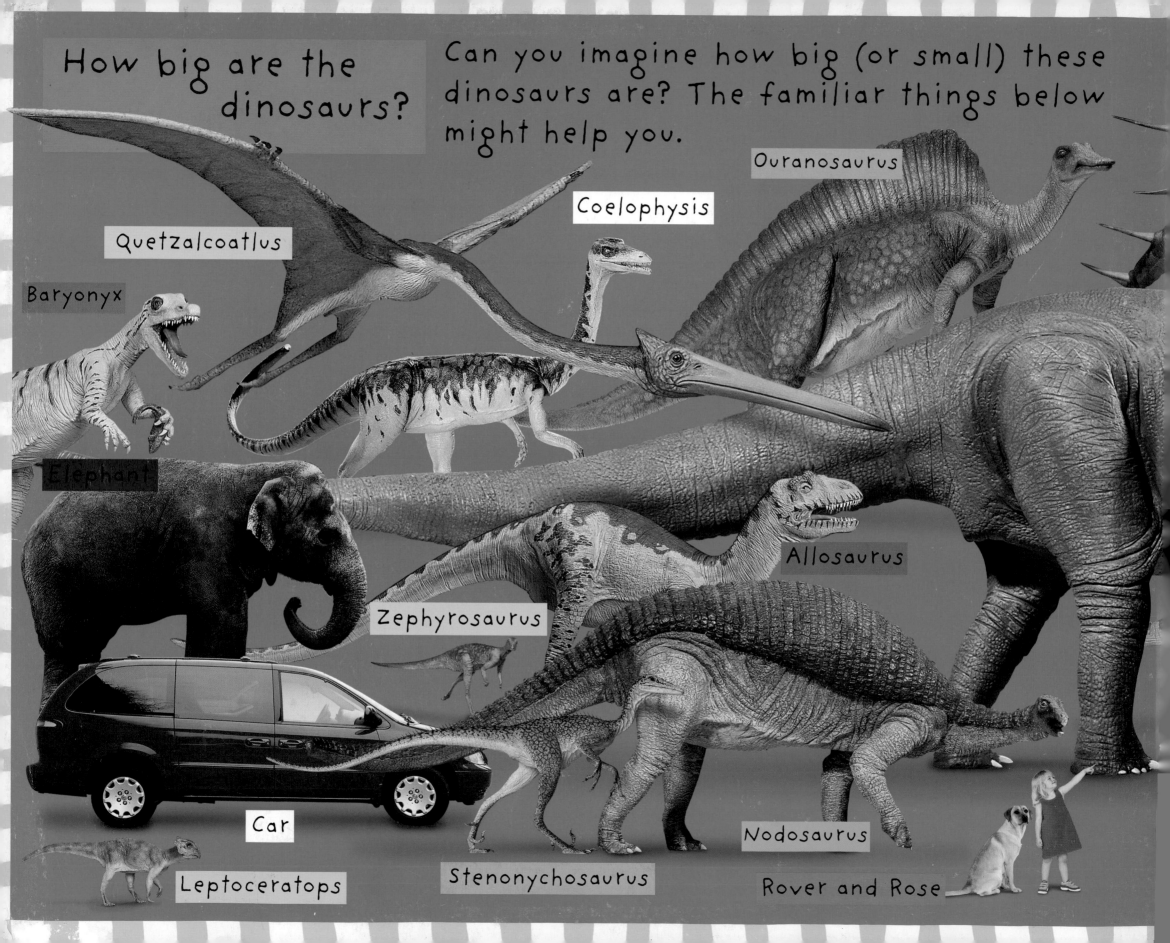